UNDER BASIL LEAVES
An Anthology of Poems

Paulette A. Ramsay

HANSIB

Published by Hansib Publications in 2010
London & Hertfordshire

Hansib Publications Limited
P.O. Box 226, Hertford, Hertfordshire, SG14 3WY, UK

Email: info@hansib-books.com
Website: www.hansib-books.com

A catalogue record for this book is
available from the British Library

ISBN: 978-1-906190-36-1

Printed and bound in the UK

Contents

Dedication

To the memory of my father, Lascelles Williams, who died too soon and to Joe Pereira, on the eve of your retirement.

"A little worm may eat a big tree."
Namibian proverb

Acknowledgements

Many persons have confirmed that they are, indeed my friends, by their willingness to read different drafts of my poems, some offering their honest comments - kind or unkind, some laughing their heads off to make me feel good about them. I thank them all.

Others who encouraged me with their enthusiasm, scepticism or questions include: Jevvor Duncan, Ellen Myers, Ingrid McLaren, Anne-María Bankay, Renisford, Lindy and Bonique.

I am grateful to Karen Clarke, Althea Aikens and Marc Ramsay for assistance with typing. Marc must be further thanked for organising the poems and for his technological support. Zac must be acknowledged for his keen eye for colours. Thanks also to Michael for his interest.

I thank Mark Wilson for the cover design. I must also express my appreciation of the time Earl McKenzie spent reading the manuscript and for his useful comments. Thanks to Professor Maureen Warner-Lewis and Dr. Mawena Logan for their help with finding some African proverbs.

Finally I must thank Arif Ali of Hansib Publications for accepting my poems for publication and for remaining committed to the project throughout the duration of the publication process. I also thank Richard Painter for his work on the manuscript.

A Few Words

Over the years, I have written many poems, many, many, more than the number in this collection. As a taciturn young girl, I wrote poems to express a range of feelings and responses to people and things. It was very easy for me to talk to paper and on paper, but I found talking to people a rather daunting and intimidating undertaking. So I wrote my words in the form of poems

The poems I wrote were all very personal and articulated my secret thoughts, moods and feelings. I wrote poems to ventilate my disdain for exasperating and meddlesome little boys in khaki uniforms, to disclose my loathing of squirming, wiggling earthworms and to make known my dread of lizards of every shape, colour and size. I wrote them and hid them. I found what I considered to be secure hiding places behind books, between books, in garment bags, underneath large stones, in dark holes in tree trunks, under flower pots and in all kinds of unexpected, secret spots, to hide my poems – my words. I seemed to be driven by the firm conviction that the ritual of writing and hiding my words would make my wishes come true. Lizards would die, worms would slither and wither away, little annoying boys in khaki uniforms would vanish out of sight and the world would become a better place.

But all of those irksome things persisted – like my nemeses – and I continued to write and hide my writing with great fervour. When I was thirteen, one of those bothersome boys in khaki uniform told me he loved my pretty little black face. I looked at his face and thought that I did not like him at all and I did not want him to like me either. So that night I wrote a poem, as a tribute to his ugly face.

At the time, I was sure that verbal musicality and rhyme were the only important elements of a poem, so I gave careful attention to these aspects of my art. I recall only the refrain of the poem which read:

You are ugly
So ugly
Ugly, ugly, ugly
Your head is so big Your face is so big
Round like the moon
I hope you die very soon.

Still hoping that my words had magical powers to make my dreams become reality, once they were put on paper, I watched that boy for months waiting for him to die. But for some reason, he did not. He just became more and more adept at unnerving me with his distasteful tricks and unwelcome overtures.

I again sought refuge in writing at sixteen, when another young man disclosed his fondness for me. He liked me very much, he declared, but thought I was too restrained and silent, so he decided to resist the romantic pull towards me. I did not tell him that I did not care two match sticks if he found me endearing or not, I just went into the quiet of my room that night and wrote a poem in which I encouraged his decision to retreat. I revelled in the thought of him taking flight as I wrote the following refrain:

Run, run as fast as you can
A ginger bread girl
Never catches
A ginger bread boy.

I loved the words and I recited them over and over in my head, hoping they would place some magical spell on him and make him permanently disappear. I saw that same young man a few months ago and smiled charmingly at him as he struggled with extremely prosaic language and crudely structured sentences, to confess to me how he rues the day he ran from me.

I eventually discovered that my hiding places were not quite so secret or secure after all. From time to time, I would glimpse a member of my family reading, or trying to read the words on a crumpled up piece of paper. No one ever said aloud that they knew who was the author of those compositions, but I suspected that they secretly held their opinions about the source of them. I however, never claimed any of them. I witnessed every public reading with indifference and successfully created the impression that I had no interest, either in the words being pronounced aloud, or in the sentiments they expressed. I was the stoic observer of a meaningless act.

I did discover one of my poems which made me think that perhaps there were times I should have kept my pencil hidden and resisted the impetus to write. It was a poem I wrote after I allowed myself to reciprocate the emotional attraction expressed to me by a bold young man. I soon found a reason to rebuff and extinguish those sentiments and conveyed my intentions with a swiftly crafted verse:

You are my beloved enemy,
I love you with all my heart
But now we must part
For no matter how much I love you
They say I cannot have you,
My beloved enemy.

I still cannot understand what unfathomable, masochistic appetite for self-denial led me to inscribe those words, but I am convinced today, they were among the words I probably should never have created at all and having been created, they deserved to be hidden without the possibility of ever being found, or of ever having any effect on anyone's reality.

The poems in this collection deal with a wide range of themes, issues and ideas which I have carried in my head for a long time. They are about history, migration, man and woman, individual agency and identity, people and their idiosyncrasies, death and its inevitability, women – their strengths and achievements and paradoxically the pain many of them still experience, despite their achievements and life and its many experiences – good and bad. At least three poems celebrate the lives of individuals who were very special to me and whose deaths brought great pain and deep feelings of loss. Several other poems give expression to the centrality of memory and the role of the past in our lives. Some of the poems for which I have a special preference, give vent to the elusiveness and complexity of that emotion called love between man and woman and the disappointments and contradictions which often problematise the relationships between them. Of course, the word and its importance to everyday living, is also given centre stage in at least two poems.

All the poems, regardless of their central thematic thrusts, convey my love for words – their sounds, their denotations and connotations. I like the meanings attached to words, and I enjoy the process of searching for that meaningful or precise word to express my thoughts. Without doubt, I refuse to rest, at times, until I find the right variety of language which words allow.

The symbols I use may be open to different interpretations, but regardless of what you think they infer, they are, testaments of how I sit and allow words to roll around in my head. Some of them reveal what I believe, some disclose what I feel, some give expression to what I question, others to what I like, and some to what I dislike. Some poems (the majority) have nothing to do with me and what I feel, like or dislike.

The short piece of prose is an example of an instance

when I had great fun creating innuendos and insinuations. It is, moreover, indicative of how a poem can evolve into prose, for it was conceptualised as a poem, but I was forced to follow its unfolding as prose. It is my pleasure to share these words with you in this collection.

Paulette A. Ramsay

HISTORY AND POLITICS

" ... no se puede vivir sin historia..."
Shirley Campbell

A Word to History

Caveat
quiet counsel
threatless warning
given in peace
an injunction
to be heeded
with prudence
stay away from my country
my home,
my nation
my people
never measure my vigilance
the censure a deadly nightshade poison
certain like your own past
calamitous
ruinous
malignant.
Never give thought to a return
or casual visit
to familiar sites
forgotten caves
gold mines
sugar cane lands.
Never consider
finding
again adventure
new rocks
new mountains
missing pirates
lost gold
lost pebbles.

Never consider righting
the cartographer's wrongs
tell him
yes him, imperialist
colonialist
self-serving
mastermind of all ill
my people have known
tell him never to return
never
cross my pristine waters
land on my sanitized shores
to (re)map
the routes already mapped
to re-route the
paths already routed
to re-uproot the roots replanted
to rewrite stories
already written
to reclaim the lands
already claimed
to unlock
chains long broken
tell him quietly
to stay away
for if he visits my shores
pretending to know me
or where I've been
or where I need to go
or how I should write my name
or tell my story
or build my home
or set my nation free
or keep my nation free
there's a new decree
I'm the new scout
the new informant

the new double agent
the rightful captain
the owner of the rock
the new surveillance officer
my vigilance is steadfast
against counter-surveillance
and counter-espionage
even in camouflage.
Tell Mr. history
the landscape is different
there is terrorism
here now
it is no longer safe
for curious explorers
and expeditioners
so
tell mr. history
to stay away
keep his story
new or old
it's the same
if he just as set foot on
the edge of my
country
I will do violence
to him
physical violence
emotional violence
he must never
walk these shores
or chart courses
in these lands
ever again
this time
I'm sure.
We've been here
a long time

and we know
his story…

Her Majesty's Seal

Someone at the British High Commission
did not agree with my express photographer
that the smile I had practiced
in front of the mirror for a whole half hour
made me look beautiful
brought out my innocence
made my lips look sexy.
He or she
had with firm prerogative
blotted out my face with
her Majesty's Seal.

The lion's head made an obscene pattern
on my forehead
his torso covered my two eyes
and his behind sat imperiously
over my nose and sexy mouth.
At least my two cheekbones
my vain claim to African royalty
stood out on either side of his torso
small assurance
I had not been totally obliterated by the beast.

It's a lie I tell myself
they have no interest in my photo
they just could not catch me
to brand my face
force me to carry the mark of the beast
in my forehead
so they stamped it on my photo instead
blotted out my face.

When I arrive at Heathrow
her Majesty's Imperial seal
in the place where my face should be
will be enough to let me
a (former) colonial subject
in.

I Would Rewrite History

For Shirley Campbell

A friend confessed to another
that she would like
to do merciless violence to history.
destroy
deconstruct
his non-Afrocentricity
obliterate him
silence him
remove his ability to silence
the true history of Africa
dismantle the foundations
of his colonial story.

She would hit him in the face
make him spit blood
swallow his Eurocentric story
choke on his Eurocentric discourse
scream a new story.

She would nail him to the map of Africa
force him to speak the truth
confess the lies he has told
she would kick him in the gut
kick his heels
knock his teeth out
prevent him from walking
from talking
lies about Africa
lies about Afro-derived people.

The friend listened

then declared
I would never render an eye for an eye.
I would simply rewrite history
tell my story.
Re-centre my African story.
Engender racial pride in black people
restore their dignity
arm them with the truth
about Africa
their past
their heritage
their identity.

I would write their story
which was from the beginning
before he wrote his version
before he falsified the truth
about their story
our story.
For the truth
will let them know themselves
understand the road ahead
tell others who they really are.

I would simply re-write history.

No Carbon Copies Allowed

modernity?
modernism?
modernize?
modern ideas?
modern methods?
forward-working approaches?
progressive attitudes?
contemporary theories?
current practices?
advancement?

What lofty agenda
a rescue mission
how coincidental
the same claims
of value
of policy
faulty
invalid
deduced from the same premise
by those who brought
slavery
colonialism
apartheid
exploitation
invasions and plundering
to Africa
the Caribbean.
Those who stood over there
somewhere...
said we were too different

we, the others
did not speak their language
wear their clothes
read their books
watch their television
with pornography
barefaced promotion of consumerism
were too different
not advanced
not modern
not *avante gard*.

It was all for our good
they would use
our gold
our bauxite
our nickel
our lumber
our banana

And in the draining process
in the one-way exchange
modernity
modernism
advancement
would come to us.

We embraced every plot
every institution
they devised or constructed
to obfuscate our own ideas
to confuse us
overwhelm us
thwart our efforts
our plans to assert our own
agency
as sovereign nations.

And now you come
with the same story
same blueprint
same plan
same agenda

It has never occurred to you
or them
or the ones before you
that we reject
your plans of altruism
their plans of altruism
your concerns for humanity
their concerns for humanity
that we embrace our difference
for we long discovered
that we do not have to be
carbon copies of you
we embrace our difference
we celebrate our difference
we exist for our difference
for heterogeneity
for diversity
for dissimilarity
in our difference
we find ourselves
we find our individual identities
we assert our subjectivity
we become self-certain
we become ourselves
we are free
of the dismantling power
of your modernity.

Inauguration Day 2009

*"Let the rivers clap their hands and let the hills be joyful
together"*

Hands
   of many hues

Minds
  of various political hues
     in resolute clasps
  Fingers entwined
       firmly
          around this day
            Apogee
            Apotheosis
            Acclamation
            Homage

The political
The apolitical
Give ear
to the encomia
plaudits
Join in exultation
of this venerated one's acme

Disown dubiety and schisms
Foment exuberance
even the
  barroque
It has begun!
  The righting
    re-writing
       writing and rewriting
         of everybody's story

America's story
the World's story
of history
everybody's history
America's history
the World's history

Here, in this Mall
in your own hall
in towns big and small
in large and sprawling cities
in diverse corners
the world over
some seek the cool
in heated climes
some take cover
in freezing times
all watch
the flame rekindle
after silent litanies
invocations
with profound reverence

Let this flame never flicker
nor fail...
all schizophrenic
before the new nomenclature
post-racial

non-racial
bi-racial
multi-racial
cross-racial
hybrid
did someone
mouth black?
Wall Street crashes
The Dow collapses

Bankers wail, declare memory lapses
But they have no care
Today
Not now
Not this moment
Suspended as they are
In time and space
by every sound
every syllable
every word
every sentence.

They will not crash
they will not collapse
even from the edge
of these words
the wails of bankers
the words of bankers
investors
pessimistic economists
will not penetrate
the euphoria
       of the children in a small town
       in Alabama
       of the children in a village
       in Kenya
       of the people on King Street
       in Jamaica
       expressions of genuine joy
       of transient foreigners
       in Victoria Station
       expressions of total amazement and awe
the euphoria of the women
       in a church in North Alabama
       expressions of reverence
       expressions of deep gratitude
the euphoria of women in Georgetown

the euphoria of men in a bar in
        Bridgetown
the euphoria of young boys
        who pause as a snapper struggles
        at the end of their lines
to listen to the words
the wind is bringing
        across the world
this is the day
this is the moment
this is the time
the day
the pages of history
turn
with our hopes
our smiles
our cheers.

Unclench your fists
clap your hands
capture this redemptive vision.
Drop the line and do somersaults
pass it on
to someone
But is there anyone
Who has not heard?
Tell them again
Tell yourself again
Say it with soberness
Say it quietly
The day has come
The word is spoken
Quietly, placidly.
Hand boldy touching
The WORD
It is done.

Summon the great poets
Where's Dereck Walcott
Where's Maya Angelou?
Langston Hughes
Now we need the blues
Gwendolyn Brooks
Would write a new book.
Listen, listen
You hear Bob Marley
With this one?
Redemption Song
Redemption word
Redemptive vision.

Investors panic
Nasdaq is erratic
But they ain't watching
That
Today they watching the
Hand on the Bible
Today they all
Celebrate
A journey's end
And beginning

We now all know
what the birds and the trees
the sharks and the seas
must know too
it has happened
it has happened
that time is no more
this time is now
we all claim this time.

Cynics
Skeptics

Believers
Supporters
Atheists
Semi-atheists
Racists
Non-racists
Political
Apolitical
It is the world's
time
to witness the
sunshine anew
its rays conceal the blot
of shame
of horror
of denial
of appropriation
of misappropriation
of hate
and shine on the face
of the son
favoured
to turn the table
this time
redemption time
like Joshua
like Moses
like David
supplications
for humility
supplications
for wisdom
… Supplications…
for strength
… Supplications
for temperance
… Supplications

for divine guidance
… Supplications
for protection
for dreams to become
real solid parts
of lives, of homes, of countries
real surreal moment.
Look, see the ancestors
the leaders
of the Harlem Renaissance
believers of Negritude
believers in the wisdom of Marcus Garvey
believers in Cesaires' cultural vision
hoping
praying
singing
in a celestial choir.
Listen, hear the chant?
Celebration
Praise
for this day
in every tongue
in every land.
You hear Bob Marley
chanting this one
Redemption song
Redemption word.

Claim this day
a new embodiment of dreams
many and varied
common dreams
shared dreams
faces with light
eyes with light
faces with smiles

smiling eyes
living their first
truly
        surreal moment
        real surreal moment.

Settle down now
You can sit now
and rest...

Rest
For today you celebrate
Tomorrow
you begin the task of finishing
the story
you start today
today is the beginning
not the denouement.

To An Erudite African Professor

If you had your way
you say
you would end all aid
to Africa, the Caribbean
every place in which people
ravaged by hunger and disease
wait with outstretched bowls and crocus bags
to receive from the over-flowing pantries
of wealthy countries.

We are too willing
you say
to accept charity
hands outstretched
lacking agency
the will
to fend for ourselves.

I say to you
Sir, with respect
I have no shame
no remorse
if those who robbed us
left us bare
in the name of civilization
are now conscience-stricken
accepting it is time to pay back
a modicum
of all things stolen.

Pay-back
is long overdue.

WORDS AND OTHER THOUGHTS

"In the beginning was the word…"

Milk to the World

yesterday
I discovered a word
     or shall I say
     stumbled
       upon a word
        lying there
between the blades of crab grass.

I picked it up with caution
held firmly in my grasp
this word
I did not know
this word
I could not know
it never crossed my path.

I examined it
touched it
smelt it
felt it
no feature of a word
was absent
I could tell
no ordinary word
in my palm
and ignorance no balm
its meaning I tried to tell
its letters I tried to spell
all in vain
its synonyms I knew not
its antonyms I guessed not

I spoke to the word
with my finger
I traced its face
its shape,
I listened to its sound
it spoke quietly
but with the force of tropical breeze
with ease
said
it was not really a word
it was the word
word of words
word to the world
sustenance for grass
distraction for me
attraction for you
a word
that was every word
a code
the centre
of every word
light
a guide
a tool
a map
a cure
food

milk for babes
milk for old men
milk for pregnant mothers
milk for dry breasts
milk for old women with withered breasts

I kept the word
to the grass
it could not return

I needed this word
to whisper sounds
I understand not
I placed the word
close to my breast.

Today,
I touch the word
I think
I remember
that only yesterday at dawn
I did not know this word
did not expect
that it would now rest
upon my breast
this word
my word
word of words
word to the world
word for the world
word
word
word
words
milk to the world

I own this word
my word
my language
the word that makes me
human
woman
alive
present
in the world
with a word
milk to the world.

When a Little Girl Grows Up

When a little girl grows up
and becomes a woman
she discovers words
plays with words
rolls them around in her hands
balls of many colours
not in the monotonous
monosyllabic way
she played with her dolls
but in complex multi-syllabic
multiplicities of multi-layered
meanings
she inspires
conspires
probes
interrogates
uncovers
discloses
exposes
tempts
loves
she spouts philosophies
and theories
feminisms
agnosticism...

She discovers genres
chooses her preferred type
writes gender equality
re- configures sex
excavates

the secret places
of men's minds
tries to pry them open
unlock complex words
and sentences in their heads.

When a little girl grows up
she discovers things
like magazines on racks
balls on playing fields
sea shells on silent sands
echoing the sounds of talkative waves
whispers of a story of endless love.

When a little girl grows up
She constructs new meanings
new words
deconstructs old meanings
creates new words
makes new connections
gives birth to new words
caresses them
nurtures them
and she will stab you in the eyes
with some sharp pointed words
if she thinks its necessary.

Alternative Discourse

Wha a gwan mi dups?
Mi deh ya my yout.
Yuh hear bout di Miggle East ting an ting?
Yu mean di Israeli Palestine ting?
Serious ting dat my yout.
Dat mi a say too.
Babylon business.
True true ting.
Freedom an justice time.
You done know.
Time fi peace.
Peace an love.
Bun out wickednis.
Nuh say nutten.

Identity Crisis

Last week
she misplaced her red wig
so she wore the pink one
the whole week.
Yesterday
she misplaced the pink wig
damn blasted own way wigs.
So today she decided to permanently weave
burgundy and pink curls onto her head.

Academic Birth Pangs

Writing an academic paper
is like giving birth
except there is no epidural
no C- section
to accelerate the agonizing process
avoid complications
bring it to a grand finale
still with pain
but perhaps a little less punishing
with the help of anesthesia
there are many accidental episiotomies
prolonged contractions
but the final push brings great delight
a living breathing essay
that speaks to the minds of many
brings gratification to a sore head
attempting to recover
even as thoughts
for the next thesis
a zygote
are fertilized.

About Regret

Regret does not understand
what people mean
when they say
life is short.

It lives forever.

WOMEN

"The proper study of mankind is woman."
Henry Adams Brooks

These Are The Women

(For Anne-María Bankay)

these are they
the women
who know
who see
who can tell
perceive
read the minds
of other women
of their children
of others

these are they
the women
who can tell
that the life
we plan
and dream of
when we are young
and starry-eyed
is but that
a dream
a nightmare
a ball of cotton
that unravels everyday
even as we burn our fingers
on hot dinners
over feeble stoves
for the family we prayed
to have
and now sometimes
wish we did'nt have

these are they
the women who know
we wouldn't trade
or betray
or disappoint
those creatures
that came from our loins
though elimination
sometimes seems
a welcome path

these are they
the women
who have lived
happy times
sad times
happy-sad times
times with money
times without money
cold
heat
rain
sunshine...
empty and warm embraces
warm and cold embraces
pointless embraces...

These are they
the women who know that
sometimes the only solution
comes from kneeling by your own bed
using the sheet to dry your eyes
and being glad
nobody saw your
tears big and wet
like the water in the bathtub which
nobody cleans but you

glad that in the end
you cannot hide from God
even when you hide from everyone else

these are the women
who tell you half- truths
half the truth
each time you ask
half the truth because
they know that
the other half
you will find
on your own
eventually
to your own shock
or surprise
or mirth
or humour
or satisfaction
or cynicism
or disappointment
or indifference
or gratitude
or ingratitude...

these are they
the women
who can make
a dollar
feed a family of five
and tithe
give to charity
and smile

these are they
the women who know
that like them

you will have to pretend
you like so many things

sometimes
all the times
some things
sometimes
all the time
some people or person
him,
her,
them,
sometimes,
all the time
this,
that,
these,
those,
in the end
it doesn't matter

these are they
the women
who are brave
in things
that do not touch
their inner core
they suffer
quietly
love sometimes
laugh sometimes
but suffer
under the scab
the markings
the superficial smile
the camouflage
they know that smile

that you think
only you can read
interpret
or
understand
they can read eyes
like those who
read palms and tea leaves
these are the women
who know what it is to be chauffeur,
nurse,
cook,
cleaner,
bathroom scrubber,
tired lover, real lover, fake lover
sometimes lover, sometimes hater...

these are the women
who know all about
rolling over in a ball
curling up
face to the wall
squeezing an infertile womb
disappointed abdomen
lonely pelvis
and praying
"Puppa Jesus
Father God
I will do this to please
you and You Only"

these are they
the women
who can safely generalize
make inductive claims
about men,
most men,

many men,
their men,
other women's men
that they know

nothing
about love
with lying lips
they perform
and well they do
the role of nice
I love you
just for that
all for the feel
of their hot places
their juices
their passions
fake or real
it's what they must take
they smile for it
display good behaviour
their bodies
controlled
they love
most men
many men
only that
women want man-love
these women know
the f—ers
imbeciles
know
nothing
about
true love.

these are the women

who have looked
at life
around corners
through periscopes
down the years
through telescopes
through eyes
into souls...
cold souls
sick souls
dead souls
kind souls
mean souls
empty souls
loving souls
they know life
they have lived life
they have felt life
travelled life
loved life
suffered life
endured life
and still
ask for more life

and they pray
and they love
God
and life
their children
and pray to love
the damn fool
they brought into their lives
an act of volition
ill calculated...they wait...
but they know
these women

that the day
will not come
when they will
no longer rue
every high-minded decision
every ill-founded act
every lost chance
every missed opportunity
every frozen moment
but they hope

for they know the gift
they have to give
love round and perfect
like the full moon
bright and illuminating
like the Sunday afternoon sun
soft like pouis petals
deep
like the Blue Lagoon
wide...
warm...
encompassing...
playful like the Caribbean Sea
tougher than coconut shell
Queen Conch's House
mystifying and beautiful...

and they wait...
            these women

Monologue of a Papine Market Vendor

Ef mi like sellin in di maakit?
What kine a question dat
You could ask mi so?
Mi love dis maakit
Me love dis likkle spat here so
More dan anyting in dis worl.

Ebry day
I wake up
I say tank you Fada Gawd
You wake mi up
For anada maakit day.
I come day afta day
Wid a smile pon mi face
You could see dis smiling face
An aks mi if mi happy in dis place?

I love dis place
Dis likkle spot
Dis likkle stool.
I love to spread out mi tings
Fi you and everybody dat come
To dis place.
Thirty years I range dem di same way
Ebry day

De yallow yam here so
De breadfruit here so
Now de punkin, bright orange colour
Go right beside de green banana.

You see de punkin bright pretty colour
Tek dis and put in a beef soup
Wid a likkle a dis tyme an skellion
Notten sweeta.
Den mi range de peppa
And de tomatis beside each odda
Mi jus love dis pitcha
Is a reel reel pitcha
A mek everyday
Like painta.
A mek pitcha
A sell from di pitcha
A smile to mi custamas.
Dem love de colorful pitcha.
Den de oranges come here so
De garden egg here so.
Is not everybody like dis one
Maybe is de purple de doant like
Funeral colour you know.

Den look now
A always put de ciniman
An nutmeg here so man
Is jus' like how you range
You table fi eat you know
You say de knife here so
De fork here so
De plate here so
You create a pitcha wid a pattaan
Same way I create a pitcha wid
A pattaan.

Mi customas love di pattaan
A sell from di pattaan
So mi sell
So mi fix bac di pattaan
Is a aat ma'am

Is designin ma'am.
A tek di Fada fruit and tings
An a design pitcha
Draw de people to mi.

Thirty years I come do dis ting
Never tiad
Never bex
How mi fi bex?
An mi get money
Feed mi family
Buy clothes fi mi family
Afta mi no fool, fool
Mi treat mi buyers right
Everyting tight.

A wonda what squeeze dis naseberry?
You like naseberry?
Is a delicate likkle fruit
A have a Indian custama
Who say is har favourite fruit
Buy it by de dozen
Green or ripe
Is jus har type.

So I tell you
A don't lie to you
Look in mi face
It will show dat a love dis place
So you buyin dis breadfruit?
It will roast an eat good
Doant you can tell?
I only sell good food
No fertiliza food
St. Elizabeth clean clean food
Grow inna good dirt
No get no spray

Everyday I pray
Lawd doan sen bad food my way
So when I pay a faama
I know him is a man of hona
I know him tell mi di truth
Him eye full a truth
So you doan fret
Nobody dead from dis food yet
Nobody will
By Gawd will.

No doan put dat dere
Dat come right here
Right here
I have de pitcha in mi head
Will remember it till ah dead
Ah really doan like people touch mi tings
Only I can range mi tings
Ef you sure you buyin
You can take it up, yes
No, dat is not dear
If you walk down de line mi dear
You fine it for twice de price of mine
An it not as fine
As mine

So ef you notice
I mek different likkle sections
Dis right here is di spice section
You see
Cinniman, nutmeg, rosemary –
You see
Ova here is de herbs section
No, doan look at me dat way
Ad doan sell dat kind a herb
Herb like tyme, mint and ram goat beard.
Dis right here is de fruit section

You can see fi youself you know
Every fruit Jamaica grow
In season
Out a season
You fine it right here in dis section
Touch de one dat is you favourite
You like june plum?
Some people doan like june plum
Say it jook, jook up dem tongue
But me like it too
You like mango too?
You is jus like me
Mi is a mango lova
Any type a mango

You see how mi range dem
De Julie
You see dose fus
Den di East Indian
What a mango fi mango lovas!
Doan bada talk bout de Bombay
A could eat dat one everyday
Mi is a true mango lova
But doctor say watch mi shuga
So I cut mi eye pass it sometimes
But sometimes mi sidung right here so
An eat a six or a five.

Den look on de vegetable section
De tomatis, de carrot, de cho-cho
Hey, a lady from Puerto Rico
Come here an tell mi dat cho-cho
Is not a word a must say loud
She say in her country is a word
You whispa ina crowd
Far it have different meaing
See ya mah, a wat kind a meaning?

You know dat meaning?
You travel to Puerto Rico?
Dem doant call it cho-cho?
What a someting
An I don't want to get into dem rude tings.

But you talking bout name?
You see dem students from over University
Dat come to dis city from de likkle islands?
I gats to teach dem our names
And I mek dem touch de tings
For I don't know de name
Dem use in Trinidad and Barbados
An dose likkle, likkle islands.

Is a joke
Deh touch mi cho-cho an say christophine
I laugh
I say cho-cho.
Deh touch mi june plum an say pommesettiere
I laugh
I say june plum.
Deh touch mi apple and say pommerac
I laugh
I say apple.
Den some a dem confuse fi true
De look at mi guinep
An call it ackee
An de look at mi cashew
And call it apple.

Ah say no, no, no
Is one ting to have different name fi di tings
But is another ting to call one ting
By di name of de oder
Ackee is ackee
cashew is cashew.

So you see how name is important
We have to know de right name
To mek sure we buy di right ting.

My grandmadda always say
You name mek you who you be
Know you name
Say you name wid pride.
Wait, see one of mi student customas.

Morning nice young man
What you buying today young man?
You buying what?
Sapodilla?
Is a likkle Trinidadian one.
I tell you all di time dat
I sell naseberry
But I understan you now man
Ah learn a new word from you man

Sometimes I joke to mi Jamaicans
An say, you want sapodilla?
You learn my words
I learn your words
You buy my fruits
I sell you fruits
An all a wi happy.
Tanks young man
Enjoy you day.

You see how it nice an easy
Selling in dis jplace
Ef I love dis place?
Look in my face
Dis is my place
Dis place keep my face
An mi fambily's face

Happy
All de time
An ef you keep di pitcha
Of this corner
In your mine
You will be happy
All di time.

What Women Don't Always Tell Men

Women don't always tell men
some little
but important things
like
by the way
that thing
you thought
was cute
was actually very ugly
and that thing you thought
was a blast
was barely a peep
for me.

And by the way
when I said
you were my knight
it was true then
and for a little while
but now
you're neither
my knight
nor bishop
nor rook...

MAN AND WOMAN

*"The woman who is known only through
a man is known wrong."*

Henry Adams Brooks

Personal Gardener

She left her husband
because he did not like gardening
her flowers and herbs withered and died
but he did not seem to care
so she married her gardener
and now she does not have to pay
to keep her plants alive.

Revelation Dream

she met him
in the conference room
such a brief encounter
but enough
to disclose
eloquence
erudition
allure

spellbound by
firm handshake
solid frame
she vowed to meet him again...

that night
she dreamt of such a meeting
once again
in the conference room
the enchantment
suddenly a cruel curse
as he painted his toenails
with polish the colour of scarlet.

Divorce Aftermath:
An Apoplectic Woman Speaks Out

Sequel to all of this:
Henceforth
Not even a plate of dinner
I buy with any of them
Ole robber!
The whole damn lot of dem
Ole wretch!
Damn tief...

Imagine he gets everything
Like is him one buy dem
Down to de cyar
The wretch is driving
With his worldly new woman
Is my money buy
Ole wretch!
Gawn wid him two han full
And running over...

I should have put that Italian sofa
outa door.
Mek sun bun it!
Mek rain wet it!
Damn tief!
The whole damn lot of dem

Look at him
Listen to him
Declare his legal rights
Listen to him
Express his abhorrence

For fights
But he bamboozle me
Ass wispy like weasel

Not one more!
Not even a passing association
Not one more
Not even a look in my direction
Jook out him two eyes dem
That way
I will never have to sign
Papers like these
Sign over my rights
To a tief
Legitimise robbery
Parasitic dunderheads!
The whole damn lot of them.

There Is No Name For A Man Who Is Bad

When I was four
I heard my mother tell Miss Millie next door
that Jenny who lived on the left side,
who always left her door open wide,
was a slub.

When I was six
in the middle of my act
of picking up sticks
I discovered a slimy mess
since my mother and I had this pact
show me everything
tell me everything
I showed her the slimy mess
it's a slug she said.
a slow, slimy slug.

So this is what Jenny is?
a slow, slimy slug
I was sure
Jenny walked so slow
past our gate
past the neighbour's gate
past Miss Dill's gate
past Miss Rob's gate
Jenny is a slug.
she so slow
slow, slow Jenny
Jenny the slug.

When I was ten

I heard my mother say
to the neighbour next door
that girl Jenny, she face so sour
she has no will power
I wonder when
she will stop being a slut.

A slug Mama, I said.
a slow slow slug.
hush, she said,
you're a girl of ten
get your book and pen
study everything ten times ten
so you will never end up like Jenny
a slut.

I took my book
and I wrote the word
S-L-U-T
I took my dictionary
and searched for this word
I read its meaning
and wondered how Jenny
could be what the dictionary said.
so I crossed the word
out of my dictionary
I did not read that word
I could not use that word
 to name Jenny.
so that word became dead.

When I was fifteen
I again heard the word I had killed
slut
my mother told Miss Millie next door
Jenny is a slut.
Once a slut, always a slut

see she done with Miss Dill's husband
she done with Miss Rob's husband
and now she's after yours
God knows whose will be next.

That night I asked my mother,
why Jenny is a slut
it's what she does
with men in the village
bad things
that's why she's a slut.

What's the word for those men?
I asked.
no word, she said.
they are men.
slut? I asked her.
no, she said.
that's a word for Jenny.

Now I am twenty one.
I understand why my grandmother always sings
puss and dog don't have de same luck.
There is no such name for a bad man
He is just a man.
Slub?
Sluth?
Slug?
Slut?
No.
Man.
Just man.

A Man Lives Here

You know a man lives here
or there
for that matter
because you see his trousers
on the clothes line.
Of course they look fine
not washed by his hands
but by those of a woman so fine.

Do not for a minute think
that the mended fence
painted walls
neatly trimmed hedge
unclogged toilets
well-kept lawns
mended faucets
paintings on the wall
well-behaved children
blooming things
are his doing at all
he has no time
for things so unsublime
not a blooming thing.   nature

After all
he is a man
a very busy man.

69

RYDAY MATTERS

*"life is a glorious cycle of song,
A medley of extemporanea ..."*

Dorothy Parker

At the Bottom of the Well

There
was
nothing
at the bottom
of
the well.
But no-one knew.

Under Basil Leaves

Mama grew a pot of basil
on her kitchen window sill
it was
she said
plant of plants
herb of herbs
spice of spices
cure of all ills
highlighter of her culinary skills
killed Granny's tumour
cured Papa's hypertension
relieved her own tension
poisoned worms
in my brother's belly.

Everyday
Mama pampered her pot of basil
on the kitchen window sill
abundant
bold shades of green
iridescent stems
florid lime green blooms
lush leaves for stews
lush leaves for brews
balm for tired crews.

Every morning
Mama
talked to her pot of basil
on the kitchen window sill.
Yesterday her blood-curdling scream

pierced the air
as her basil fainted
under her familiar touch
lush luxuriant leaves
clinging like wounded birds
to her fingers
her scream intensifying
as swift search uncovered
a portly worm
lethargic
after feasting all night
on the succulent roots
of her beloved basil.

To an Annoying Mosquito

mosquito…
little mosquito,
tiny mosquito,
your ways I know not well
but hear me well,
give heed to my voice,
my advice
take closely…
stop buzzing in my ear
this is a new year.
stop trying to sink
your little dart
into my skin
ears, nose and chin.

listen to me
closely
I'm calm
very calm
rubbing my right arm
but this
my final word to you.
I don't care
if you
are only
a zillionth zillionth
the size of my right palm
I don't care
if you need,
desire
or crave blood

for your eggs
potential
real
existing
soon-to-be-existing
whatever
your need
imagined
or real
I don't give a damn!
If you bore
a tiny hole
in the mole
in my forehead
or in my left or
right cheek
in any part of my smooth skin
I will not create a din
for I am calm
very calm
but I will slap you
with my right palm
and bust your
tiny ass.

Reverse Migration

Thanks nine eleven
I don't mean I take pleasure
in America's tragedy and misery
but you gave me the excuse,
the reason
I've searched for, for years
to go home.
I can look anyone in the eyes now
and declare my deep fear of a recurrence
of September 11 events.

Even my mother's arch enemies on the church choir
will understand.
who woulda want fi tan in a place like dat Ma?
No sah, it no safe, at all.
betta she come home Miss Jana
she safe right yah suh.

I can go home now
no need
to find reasonable arguments
to defend
my views
about alienation
estrangement
outsider status
racial discrimination
cultural exclusion
minority status.
What the hell are those?

My grand uncle went to England
lived there for forty years
worked as the only black bloke
In a factory for six years
spoke to not a single West Indian
for more than two years
never complained about cultural alienation
never complained about psychological terror
never complained about outsiderness
never complained about racism
never complained about discrimination
he just kept sending large sums of
pounds to my grandaunt
who bought milk and beef
fed her children
until he came home in a box
smelling of varnish and formaldehyde.
so which family member
would understand my claims?

I'm going home now
alive and sane
I tell everybody
you wouldn't want to live there
not after nine eleven
they say is true,
true, true.

America is a place
to run way from now.

Church Matters

She knelt meekly at the altar
bowed her head and prayed silently
then as if to a cue
she lifted her hand
stretched forth her palm
to accept the offer
of the body broken in
her stead
symbol of supreme sacrifice
she chews with reverence
and gratitude
swallows with dignity
bows her head and prays again
she lifts her head
accepts the offer
of the blood shed in her stead
symbol of supreme sacrifice
she swallows with gratitude
happy to be among
the chosen ones
her prayer of gratitude completed
her ritual of holiness ended.

She rises from the altar,
cuts her eye and
twist-up twist-up her mouth
at Angie as she passes her
on her way
to receive her own
emblems of sacrifice and love.

Ode to the Ant

little ant
remarkable creature
phenomenal being
worker exemplar
unlikely friend
quick foe

how you mesmerize
with your neat plan
your tireless
pursuit
of food
of work
of gain
for your multitudinous clan
no crumb
daunts you
with its size
no task
unnerves you
with its complexity
I should learn from you
be like you
bold

fearless
relentless
but wary of man
who will take life
in a second.

Window to your soul

your unperturbed face
creaseless
though in perpetual smile
may be
a peace offering
a reflection of your
inner serenity
I can never be sure
the wide grin
thoughtful eyes
softly quivering lips
may tell
or hide
your thoughts
innocent dreams
sinister plots
fondness for me
hatred
tell me
I cannot guess.

Perhaps I should
concur with
Shakespeare
your face
a wall is static always
unyielding
unrevealing
no window to your soul.

When the Yellow Pouis Bloom

The sun
can go to sleep
rest
in any corner
where yellow pouis
bloom
          spread
their golden feathers
like a million
suns shattered
their golden rays
          scattered
illuminating
every corner
brightening smiles
cooling hot anger
evoking dreams
making eyes twinkle with glee
as each petal
glows
a golden yellow
          shimmering
sparkling
like new gold.

Pioneer

you
are indeed a pioneer

you were bold,
adventurous
intrepid
valorously presumptuous
shameless.
You entered
discovered
explored
places never before considered
you touched things and places
never before seen or handled
like this and that
… here
and right there…

Still Laughing

I lost my laugh yesterday
for a little while,
as I tripped over an unruly weed.
I panicked when I realized
it left me sore.
So I tried to find it
as I saw a hummingbird
try to soar,
but fall and bump its head.
I tried to find it
as I watched a lizard chase the neighbour's cat
I never imagined I would ever witness that.

Then I searched frantically
in the faces of old ladies
who had long lost theirs
it seemed.
I searched in the faces of little girls
who had not yet learned to laugh at themselves.
When I thought it was lost forever
you appeared around the corner
and now,
I am still laughing
as I remember
your face
your smile
your laughter
your inflamed kiss.

Narcissist

yesterday after
witnessing
your fame
the ease
completion
the artless
guileless
way
with which you
beguile
win over affection
attachment
partiality
i accepted that
the world
my world
which may never choose
an authentic narcissus
for a bouquet
would fawn
over you
(a narcissist)
blinded by
your sophistication
your friendliness
your courtesies
indulgence
and prosperity
the growth
of your fiery red
and green colours

your faulty petals
prevarications
spurious truths
your open double-faced mockery
of womanhood
of virtue
your counterfeit illustriousness
your fraudulent beauty
in my decadent days
i dreamt
of becoming You

now
after my redemption
my partiality to marigolds
and bougainvilleas
green grass
the flame of the forest
red clay and brown humus
i want to be
me
wide open
accommodating like the sky
i love to gaze at.

Succubus

How many times have I
watched you
to be startled anew
by your
phantasmal machinations
your credible fabrications
only to let
you breathe
in my face
my nostrils
inhaling your disarming poison
to believe you again.

How many times
have I watched
you
suck the blood from
my guts
my tender places
leave me half-dead
but still believing
still allowing you leverage
still regarding
your treacherous pietistic preaching
with misguided levity
with wonder
simplicity
and awe...

I am the
world

pointed to you
your winning
saintliness
your creepy devotion
variegated disembodiment
your breath alone
kills the plants
that make me
breathe.
Yet I allow you
to come and
go as you
please.

FAMILY

"A family is like a forest, when you are outside, it is dense; when you are inside, you realize that each tree has its place."

Proverb from the Ewe and Mina people of Togo, Benin and Ghana

My Brother

My brother died
from a cancer they couldn't find
though they knew it was there
somewhere...
and we cried
how we cried
because of the poison
no one could find...

It wormed its way
through the secret spaces in his body
set up its own network
of poisonous connections
and not a doctor had a notion
of a single cure that would work

They watched the decay
as the cancer ate its way
through and through
we held him, paper thin
felt his bones under his skin
dreading the day
he would slip away
we gave him hope with our lies
while we watched death in his dull eyes.

When he got weaker
we took him to America
promised him
the best machines were there
promised him

they could cure him there.
The doctors sighed in despair
they were the best
but could not face the test.

He was paper thin
nothing left inside of him.
He got weaker
we took him to Cuba
he would be fine
they cure that disease all the time.
They took him,
paper-thin
put him in a coffin
and said to us,
bury him.
Let him rest in peace
we cannot revive the deceased.
We took him home
buried skin and bones
beside our mother.

For his epitaph we wrote
not a famous quote
but a thought we learnt at home
"We're sorry we made you suffer."

The Family Firm

My two grandmothers formed
a two-woman firm
and together
they cured all forms of illnesses,
afflictions and maladies
of my cousins, siblings
aunts, uncles,
the whole village.

Every bruised knee
running nose
running eye
running belly
bloated belly
loss of appetite
sore gum
necessitated a trip
to one or the other.
For one had the cure
for blood and skin problems.
The other the cure
for eyes, nose and throat
belly and lung problems.

Their instruments were their eyes
Sharp, piercing, probing.
They spun us in all directions
studied our eyes
pressed our ear lobes
poked us in the ribs and cheeks
made their diagnosis

and gave us medicine
from their medicine chests.

Cool soothing
sticky ointments
green and brown liquids
all created from plants
they pulled from their gardens.
A serious illness
could mean
ginger and lemon grass
or guinea hen weed, cerasse
or tamarind leaves
arrow root or aniseed tea.
They had a bush or grass
or leaf for every illness
and when we swallowed
bitter aqueous substances
we doubted not once
that our bellies
would soon feel good
when we gritted our teeth
as stinging crushed leaves
or peppery powder was
spread on our sores
we believed
we would be healed
soon, soon
and when we could run
skip and play hopscotch
We knew that they
had healed us with
magical medicines
from their gardens.
And we believed
that one day we could
be just as they were

doctors with healing potions
but we never learnt their secrets
never had their touch.
never studied their plants
and so we tell the story
that they were the
best doctors we
ever knew.

Wedding Blues

Her son
the Oxford graduate
with the plum-in-the mouth accent
filled the cathedral with his academic equals
plus his bride's lily white extended family...

she, befuddled, fidgets in the pews
not quite understanding
the absence of some familiar faces
faces of cousins, aunts and uncles
counts
her brother
her sister
her son's father.
Perhaps they miscalculated the time
but sweet recollections of weddings
meetings and greetings
sweet reunion
help to while the time away.

Her anxiety knew no bounds
she scanned every pew with x-ray eyes
they were absent,
the ones who had wiped his nose,
the ones who had fed him,
given him spare pennies,
prayed for him
God keep him safe and sound
at Oxford,
bless him mind
missing

she struggled against the hollowness
creeping up her insides
a sick suspicion
they may not be late,
just unbidden guests.

She watched the hands of the clock
tick-tock forward
heard quiet whispers
of polite guests
animated greetings
searched the audience
again and again
inquiring eyes like laser beams
trying to find
Aunt Liz, Uncle Roy,
people of her kind
people of her son's kind
those who gave him his first toy
those who rocked him to sleep
while she worked overtime.

The first chords of the wedding march
brought her to her feet
to acceptance
they will not come
her belly
now a ball of entangled ligatures
pride pushes its head
through her fine new fancy hat
the boy shame of his people
shame of people who feed him
rock him cradle
watch him grow
dress him sore.

She catches the first big tear

in the new embroidered handkerchief
gathers her expensive leather handbag
bought just for today
stuffs shame and anger deep into it
and leaves through a side door
as her son's
lily white Oxford bride
strides
up the aisle

she quietly asks the driver of the rented Bentley
to drive her home
to hide her shame
and weep
for the loss of her son
his rejection of his own
the shame he brought to her
for how she could never look
kin and kind
in the eyes again.

Death of a Son

The boy drops his school bag to the ground
hops skillfully on to the cane truck
pulls the long thick stalk
from the tightly-packed stack.

Mr. Dennis will not lose a penny
for this
he jumps from the truck
with his sweet juicy loot
the sound of his exploding skull
reaches the ear of his mother
forty chains away
sometimes the sounds in this
quiet village are sudden and loud
maybe a truck blew a tire
or a tractor ran over an empty juice box.

She resumes her cooking
she must have dinner ready
when her son returns from school.

LOVE AND MEMORY

*"Where love rules, there is no will to power; and where
power predominates, there love is lacking.
The one is the shadow of the other."*

Carl Jung.

Thornbird

" How on earth are you ever going to explain in terms of chemistry and physics so important a biological phenomenon as first love?" Albert Einstein.

you are
my
thornbird
my singular
source of rapture
now
as you were
in the beginning
the one
I see
amidst a flock
of a thousand
others
I am
your
forever
birdwatcher
from the edges
of cliffs
from the banks of rivers
from the margins of circles
I watch
as you soar
spread your wings
dodge
cumbersome clouds
glide
through blue skies
teasingly
brush the top of trees
dally

with frolicking winds

I watched you
as a girl
caught you in her net
and wished
I could
get my net
high enough
just so
your wings
or toes
or beak
would be trapped
in it.
I could touch you then
stroke your feathers

I watched
as others
more skilful
trapped you
briefly
even in broken nets
once I heard
a catapult's
stone
brought
you
  to
    the
      ground
you healed yourself
and flew
away
before I got to you.

Sometimes
I'm sure
you're headed
straight
toward my outstretched hands
I wait for you
to flap your wings
and land
on my hands
on my shoulder
even on my head
but as you
get close to me
you soar
high
above my head
and seek
refuge
in the clouds
again and again.

Sometimes
I stand
and wait
for
close to forever
I think
some ill-fate
has befallen you
but as
hope creeps to
my toes
you suddenly
soar
above my head
perform a
magical display

of aviation tricks
just to say
it seems
I'm alive
and then you
disappear again
on some urgent
unspoken
mission.

Sometimes
I think
you do not really
see me...
I make myself
believe
you do
but often
I suspect you do not like
To fly so low.

Sometimes
I watch
as you
fly
back and forth
busily
disappearing
and appearing
from beneath
clouds
which seem to conspire
with you
to conceal
secret headquarters
sometimes
...you seem

to fly in and out
of the
rainbow
I
wish to
climb
and
slide
across.

I've seen you
land on the shoulders
of others
taller
stronger
bigger
more colourful
even as you
fly above my
outstretched hands.
I watch you
now
and
smile
take pleasure
in seeing you
soar
ride the winds
dodge the clouds
fly above my head
make me believe
you see my outstretched hands
fly around me
away from me
show the strength of your wings
making me think
one day

I could climb on them
and fly with you away
from the edge
of the cliff.

I Remember When

I remember when
my village was the Garden of Eden
we romped and rolled around in the big den
we were all owners
or rather the grown ups were
we children reaped,
"You can pick anything
except mi mint bush"
Miss Millie would shout.

we picked red, yellow, purple blossoms
from her shoe black bush
marigold and lady slippers
adorned our hair with little bouquets
plucked rose petals and sprinkled them
frightened shame-ol-ladies,
along our paths.

I remember when
my village was an orchard
we were all planters
or rather the men and women tended
watered, manured
we children reaped
ate the first, second and third fruits
we bit into their firm skins
succulents, drupes, berries
juice oozing through our fingers
down to our elbows.

"Pick anything except mi Julie Mango"

Miss Sybil would say
we remembered our manners
thanked her and moved on
to Miss Dill's Otaheti apples

and I remember when my village
was a playing field
safe, secure, sheltered
from evil
we were all innocent
lost in gaiety
oblivious to harm, and suffering
we all played
and the grownups, cheered

we never saw him
lurking in the background
the monster that would change our village
rob us of its Arcadian charm

"Careful how you walk through de ball ground",
Miss Dasa shouts now
as we sit
and remember
our village
the way it used to be.

Real Flowers

when I was a little girl
I often picked golden marigolds
in my neighbour's wide open field
a cows' pasture
sometimes
early in the morning
when they were still wet with dew
sometimes
at midday
when they glowed in the golden sunlight
morning or midnight
I tied them in little bundles
pretended I was a flower girl
and danced to the music in my head
holding them close to my face
pictured myself
carrying them
to church
on Harvest Sunday
to school
on Monday morning...

But always
ended up
discarding them
with a secret wish
they were daffodils instead
or tulips
or daisies
the ones I saw in books
the ones I yearned for

real flowers.
Now
I deeply despise flowers
that only live in books.

Going Back

"Praising what is lost makes the remembrance dear".
William Shakespeare, *All's Well That Ends Well*

when I returned
to the place I had carried in my head
such a long time
I squeezed myself
into the tiny space
chagrined...
somehow I remembered it
differently...

When I was a little girl
it was a vast playing field
now the bench
can hardly hold my book.

When I returned
to the place I had carried in my head
for such a long time
complacent dust stirred
tickled my nostrils
cottony cobwebs clouded my vision
I struggled to see in the dark
somehow
I remembered it
differently
when I was a little girl
it was a bright sunny garden
now the rays of the sun
barely penetrate the cloud of gloom
hanging over it.
such a funny thing it is...
remembering.

My Dead Knight

On a moonlight night
You said you would be my black
Knight
On a moonlight night
I said I would be your black
Queen
You said let's make a wish
I said you're my wish

You said my skin was black
Like night without moon
I said your skin was shiny and black
Like ackee seed
We were happy indeed
And the children came and played
In the moonlight and sang our song
And made us kiss
Delicious bliss
They sang our song
And made us sing songs
We got our wish

You said my skin was
Smooth as coconut jelly
I said your arms were hard
like coconut shell
they did me well
I said it with much aplomb
You said my breasts were
Soft and sweet like honeycomb
You said it with such aplomb

I said your chest
was a large firm pillow
It served me well
cradled my head
 made me rest
We said we passed the test
Till death do us part
Let us kiss
This is such bliss

You said my passion
Burned like logwood flames
Like the red
On the head
Of a woodpecker
Fiery but pleasing
Like scotch bonnet pepper
We said let us burn together

In our hot passion
Forever.

That was yesterday
Today I say
Now we can part
For death has visited us
In all parts
Death
Has brought in different parts
Empty space
White silence
Hollow words

Ashes to ashes
Dust to dust
You are dead
This is dead

This is death
Now we must part
Forever
Goodnight
Goodbye
Adiós
Dead knight.

LIFE AND DEATH

*"The world's a bubble; and the life of man, less than a
span...What then remains, but that we still should cry,
Not to be born, or being born, to die."*

Francis Bacon, *The Life of Man*

When They Laid My Father Down

ashes to ashes
dust to dust
from dust we all are
to dust shall we all return
they said

then they placed my father in the ground
for the worms to eat his body
the earth to suck his flesh and bones dry
they said I should not cry
but I did cry
and my eyes I could not dry
though they said
angels were there
waiting
to keep him
and take him
to his Creator.

If I Have My Way

I will not stop for death.
I never want to stop for him.
Whether I'm driving slow or fast
walking in the park
weeding my geranium bed
or writhing in pain in bed
if I find myself in his path
I will just let him pass.
But if I have my way
I will not stop for him at all...

If I had my way
I would never stop for him
I would just wave him along...

Eulogy Interrupted

Zebediah
sat up straight
in his coffin
back stiff like ramrod
voice loud
racous and rasping
told Miss Zilpha
shut her damn blasted mouth
about
how his life was wonderful and meaningful
how he did things his way
played his own music
and danced to it
what the blasted hell she know
about dropping dead
at age forty
two weeks after
he got the promotion he always wanted
one week after Susie promised him
her virginity
to coincide
with the end of his virginity
that said
he flopped back
down into his coffin
and slammed the lid shut.

For Jaime

*"If death has come and not yet gone away, you don't tell it,
'I'm still here.'"* Tshi proverb

I read the poem today again
Jaime,
the one you inscribed in my head
and on my heart.

How many times have I read it
before
and didn't even let you know
I'd discovered you'd written it
so effortlessly
the first day you wheeled
into my class and into my
heart?

You wrote it without worrying
about syntax
or register
or diction
the smooth spinning of your wheelchair
was your paradigm for writing.

You couldn't find the word
disease
in your dictionary
so it wasn't in your poem
you didn't need the
meaning anyway.
It didn't affect your
competence
in matrices
logic

or
ordering syllogisms.
You knew how to
avoid every fallacy
just as you knew how to steer
a wheel chair
along winding and straight paths
up and down ramps and when
there were no ramps.

I read the poem, again
Jaime
it flowed naturally
the same way you wheeled your way
in and out of my classes
across the campus
on the ring road to the library's only ramp.

I read the poem
again Jaime.
the one you said I
should read to students
about life
of how they should cherish it
and hold it
and love it
and live it.

The one about dreams
of how they should dream
of fortitude
determination
aspirations
and will of steel.

I'll read the poem
for them Jaime

and let them know
that you wrote it for
them too.

That's how I know
that you were wrong
when you said you wanted to
be a writer – one day.

You were a writer, Jaime
for you are the
author of this poem
that I now read
you wrote it ever so
quietly.
Ever so calmly
in indelible ink
in my heart
and in my head.
And this paper, like
your mother's arms
your sister's heart
will never let you or your poem
roll away
in your empty wheelchair...

We'll read this poem
over and over and over
again Jaime.

This poem...
Your poem...

Your life...

Requiem for Noel

"Many days are overcome by one death." Sukuma Proverb

My friend died and they said I should not cry
Not mourn the empty spaces
on the choir,
on the park bench,
the silence at the other end of line
each time
I forget
and dial for sharing time.
If I cry
they say I will bring shame,
to his name.

Think of his fame
they say
Do not seek to blame
or make this a game
of winners and losers.
But I tell them I am the loser
My friend has died
Believe me
I have tried
Everyday I try
But still I cry
For my friend died
While I refused to say goodbye
angry at his defiance
We were supposed to dance.

I will try
I will try
Try

to keep my eyes dry.

But who will speak the words
of comfort
of wisdom
of patience
of cheer
of promise
of hope?
You they
Say
He left you to
Speak the words he taught you.

I accuse no-one
I wanted to ask God
But heard their warning
Bow before the Sovereign One
Question not the Sovereign One
This is no game
Of winners and losers
All my loss
They simply toss
On a wave of oblivion
Like the memories of my friend
They leave
Far
On an imaginary horizon

My friend died
After his body boiled
and festered
Inside
With a cruel cancer
That dug deep into his gut
There was never any sign of a cut
a carcass full of bile

And all the time
he wore an anaemic smile
Beguiled me
Pretended he was almost whole
Just needed time to mend
Told me to smile
And hold my chin high
Watched everyday as I made sigh after sigh
Believing that in only a while
He would lift me up to the sky
With words

His powerful words
Many he spoke
At all times
In season
Always with great reason
He died with a broken smile
You must be brave
Do not see him in the grave

They say he is in heaven
They say cancer and its vile
Poison
Cantankerous carnivorous cell-eating
Tissue-tearing fangs
Cannot enter there
He's safe there
In a new and perfect form
It's the norm
Life and death
Life and decay
Resurrection
Triumph
Life
New and endless

They say now I can smile
My friend sleeps for a long while
Some say
Rejoicing in heaven
And he's fine forever
He sleeps forever
But one day he will speak
Again
Powerful words
In my dreams
In my sleep
He will dance when I dance
He will laugh when I laugh
For he wants me to try
Not to cry

I will try
I will try
For they said
My friend smiled a whole smile
And said 'see you in a little while'.

Remembering Dorothy Scott

*"It is the dying time the tall boy writes counting the
dead..."* Velma Pollard, *Leaving Traces*

colleague
counselor
mentor
friend
lady
with dainty dancing feet
lady
of style, gentility and grace,
lady
of subtlety
lady
of immense creativity
laconic but succinct
enigmatic but amiable
ethereal but impregnable
we remember you as we write
we write in memory
of your love
of words
we write to preserve your words
just as our memories of you
are indelible
on the pages of
our minds.

For Michael Jackson

"What you love, death also loves." Twi proverb

We heard you sing
your voice
quintessential
our hearts leapt
sang
clapped wildly
to your intonations
obliterating all other sounds
dulcet
euphonious.

We watched you dance
on your toes
in mid air
piroutte
body curled in myriad forms
and our spirits
twirled instinctively
in awe.

You gave us a song
for every need
every want
every thought
decibels compelling
lyrics irresistible
smoother than silk.
Today
you stopped singing
stopped dancing
left behind a wounded world

where the stones try to thrill us
with echoes of your voice.

We'll seek solace in your songs
eternal legacy
guarding the quiet knowledge that
no-one can ever put together again
the zillion pieces
into which your sudden stubborn silence
ripped our hearts
and souls
forever

We'll listen to your songs again
and again
and wait for resurrection morn.

"The Day I Rode on His Bicycle"

I said I didn't like him. He said he didn't like me. I said he was insignificant, invisible. He said I was ugly, haughty, obnoxious. I would walk right by him and not see him. He would walk right by me and not see me. Or so we pretended. I would peep at him from the corner of my eyes and I would see him do the same. If he saw me peep at him through the corner of my eye I do not know. He never made it seem as if he did. When we passed on the corridors he would put on the face of a pitiful puppy and once I saw him I put on the face of a fierce pit-bull or pit-heifer. He knew I would growl and snap if he ever approached me and so he kept his distance. I reveled in my own pretense and I enjoyed every moment watching him or peeping at him. He only needed to whimper to complete the picture, but if he ever attempted to ever show any sign of bravery, I started to prepare my voice to bark and snap.

One day, he seemed to decide he wasn't afraid of pit-bulls and so he sidled cautiously up to me and asked in a voice that was barely audible, "How comes your pleats are always so straight and neat?"

"I starch and iron them everyday," I said in my crispest voice. And then, we looked at each other in surprise. We knew what we were thinking – I/she didn't snap at me/him. She was a little aloof yes, but I still have my head on. We looked at each other, wide-eyed, said nothing and moved on. I saw him smile from the corner of my eyes. He saw me smile from the corner of his eyes. We held our heads high and moved on.

Two weeks later he moved closer to me with the same wise caution, but this time he said my name, "Dawn, how comes your hair is always so neat?" I looked up at him quickly, looked away and then looked at him again. "I comb it and brush it everyday." He didn't say, "Oh!," as if he just got information he could never think of for himself. He never said, "Really?" as if he approved of how I brushed my hair everyday. He just smiled a little at the corners of his mouth and left, walked on. He never asked me any more questions for a long time.

We continued to pass each other without seeing each other. I peeped at him through the corners of my eyes and saw him peep at me through the corner of his eyes. I always smiled through my pit-bull/pit-heifer mask. I pretended he was invisible, he pretended I was ugly, obnoxious.

When we were in Sixth form, he stopped by my desk one day and said, "Your skin is black and soft and smooth."

"Soft?" I said in a not too soft voice, "you felt it?"

"It looks soft," he said and moved away quickly.

"You don't want to know how it looks so soft?" I asked mockingly.

"How?" he asked daring me to reply..

It was finally time to attack. "You're a stupid boy," I snapped.

He just went to his desk. Maybe he couldn't find anything that was neat or soft and smooth to ask me about so he went back to passing me and peeping at me from the corner of his eyes for the rest of the term.

One day in the summer I saw him standing at my Aunt's gate with a brand new bicycle. It was beautiful and shiny like he had spent the whole two weeks cleaning it. He just stood there like he was holding a trophy for everyone to see.

I put on the best high heel steps I could do in my sneakers and stopped in front of him, "How come your bicycle is so pretty?" I asked in my most innocent sounding voice.

"I polish and shine it everyday," he said.

"Oh," I said, "that's nice.'

I was turning to repeat my best high-heel walk in my

sneakers when he said ever so matter-of-factly, "Would you like a ride?"

"Yes," I shocked him with my response.

I fixed my pleats and sat daintily on the bar.

"Where are we going?" I asked.

"Nowhere, it's just a ride," he said. We floated over the road. He didn't fall into any potholes or run over any bumps. And if he could peep at me through the corners of his eyes, he would see my grin getting wider and wider and he would ask me maybe, "How come your grin is so wide?"

And I would say, "This bicycle ride is so nice it makes me want to grin and grin."

He rode to the corner and turned slowly and rode right back to where I saw him first and stopped.

"It was a nice ride," I said.

"Yes," he said and got back on his bicycle and rode away. And then I lifted my skirt above my knees and pulled up my pleats and skipped home. I didn't have to keep my pleats so neat anymore.

women & nature

worms, America & death
　　　└89, 76, 72

Alienation of black people